THIS LAND CALLED AMERICA: WEST VIRGINIA

CREATIVE EDUCATION

Published by Creative Education
P.O. Box 227, Mankato, Minnesota 56002
Creative Education is an imprint of The Creative Company
www.thecreativecompany.us

Design by Blue Design (www.bluedes.com)
Art direction by Rita Marshall
Book production by The Design Lab
Printed in the United States of America

Photographs by Alamy (Pat & Chuck Blackley, Daniel Dempster Photography,
Danita Delimont, Thomas R. Fletcher, Andre Jenny, William S. Kuta), Corbis
(Bettmann, W. Cody, The Corcoran Gallery of Art, Richard T. Nowitz, Neal
Preston), Dreamstime (Eei_tony, Shootalot), Getty Images (Sam Bassett,
Daniel J Cox, Cameron Davidson, Ferguson & Katzman Photography/Halo
Images, Hulton Archive)

Library of Congress Cataloging-in-Publication Data
Hanel, Rachael.
West Virginia / by Rachael Hanel.
p. cm. — (This land called America)
Includes bibliographical references and index.
ISBN 978-1-58341-801-7
1. West Virginia—Juvenile literature. I. Title. II. Series.
F241.3.H36 2009
975.4—dc22   2008009531

First Edition
9 8 7 6 5 4 3 2 1

This Land Called America

WEST VIRGINIA

Rachael Hanel

West Virginia

RACHAEL HANEL

THE RISING SUN EDGES UP OVER ROLLING
HILLS COVERED WITH TREES. IN A SMALL
WEST VIRGINIA TOWN, A LINE OF MEN AND
WOMEN REPORT FOR WORK IN A COAL MINE.
AN ELEVATOR TAKES THEM HUNDREDS OF FEET
UNDER THE GROUND. THEY STEP OUT OF THE
ELEVATOR. BRIGHT, ARTIFICIAL LIGHTS SHINE
ON THE DARK WALLS AND CEILING OF THE
CAVERN IN FRONT OF THEM. FOR THE REST OF
THEIR SHIFT, THESE WORKERS WILL DIG COAL
FROM THE ROCKY EARTH. THIS IS A DANGEROUS
JOB. BIG MACHINES CAN BREAK. SOMETIMES
A ROOF COLLAPSES AND TRAPS MINERS
UNDERGROUND. BUT THE GOOD PAY KEEPS
WORKERS COMING BACK.

YEAR

1671   Explorers Thomas Batts and Robert Fallam claim the Ohio River Valley in western West Virginia for England.

EVENT

A Rich History

WEST VIRGINIA HAS ALWAYS BEEN MARKED BY TREE-COVERED MOUNTAINS AND FLOWING RIVERS. THOUSANDS OF YEARS AGO, ADENA AMERICAN INDIANS FARMED THE LAND. THEY BURIED THEIR PEOPLE IN EARTHEN MOUNDS. LATER, THE SHAWNEE, TUSCARORA, AND DELAWARE TRIBES MOVED IN. BUT BY THE 1640S, IROQUOIS FROM THE NORTH AND CHEROKEE FROM THE SOUTH HAD DRIVEN

out most other tribes. These Indians did not live in the area but used the land for hunting.

White explorers first entered West Virginia in the late 1600s. They were looking to expand the North American fur trade. In 1671, Thomas Batts and Robert Fallam claimed the Ohio River Valley in what is now western West Virginia for England. A few years later, French explorers also claimed the Ohio Valley. England regained the area after defeating the French at the end of the French and Indian War in 1763.

The first permanent settler in West Virginia was Colonel Morgan Morgan. In 1731, he built a house in Bunker Hill, in the eastern part of the state. But because much of the land was

Several American Indian tribes (opposite) took sides during the French and Indian War (above), fighting with the French against England.

YEAR

1731   West Virginia's first permanent settler, Morgan Morgan, builds a home in Bunker Hill.

EVENT

- 7 -

Harpers Ferry (pictured in 1863) was the site of a federal armory, a place where the U.S. government stored many weapons.

State bird: cardinal

Harpers Ferry

used by the Shawnee for hunting, few white settlers joined Morgan in West Virginia. Not until 1774, when the Shawnee gave up their land, did more people come to the area.

West Virginia was part of the state of Virginia when Virginia was admitted to the United States in 1788. But conflicts between east and west soon grew. Those living in eastern Virginia tended to be wealthy. They were slaveholders and lived on large farms called plantations. The west was marked by small farms and light industry. Travel was difficult in the west due to poor roads, and Virginians there didn't think they were taxed fairly. People in the west generally opposed slavery.

One of the most famous anti-slavery events occurred in Harpers Ferry (in what would become West Virginia) in 1859. A man named John Brown formed a small army. His followers planned a war to fight slavery. They stole weapons from a federal building and killed many people. Several members of Brown's army were killed in return. Brown was captured. He was hanged on December 2, 1859. Many people think this event helped start the Civil War.

Virginia broke away from the U.S. in 1861 at the beginning of the Civil War. Virginians in the west remained loyal, though. They decided to form their own state. West Virginia was granted statehood on June 20, 1863, making it the 35th state.

YEAR

1774 · After losing Lord Dunmore's War, American Indians agree not to hunt east of the Ohio River.

EVENT

West Virginia's population remained low until after the Civil War. Then, in the 1870s, transportation improved. Businesses were attracted to the new state. Immigrants from other countries settled there. Railroads helped people move around the state and connected West Virginia to important cities in other states.

Coal had been discovered in West Virginia in 1742, but it was not until after the war that the coal industry expanded greatly. The railroad helped the coal industry prosper. In the late 1800s, immigrants from southern and eastern Europe supplied much of the mining labor.

Other important industries grew as well. Oil and natural gas were extracted from the ground. Logging supplied vast amounts of wood, leaving behind treeless hills. With its abundance of natural resources, West Virginia was poised to become an important state in the 20th century.

The railroads that brought people to work and live in West Virginia (above) also carried resources such as logs (opposite) out of the state.

A Scenic Place

West Virginia is known as "The Mountain State" because it has the highest average elevation of any state east of the Mississippi River. The state is shaped like an oval, with two narrow strips of land sticking out. These "panhandles" stretch out to the east and north. The state's western boundary is formed by a nearly 300-mile (483 km) stretch

of the Ohio River. On the other side of the river lies Ohio. To the north and east, West Virginia is bordered by Pennsylvania, Maryland, and Virginia. Kentucky is to its southwest.

Creeks wind through state parks (above) as well as mountainous areas such as those near Spruce Knob (opposite).

West Virginia lies within a region known as the Appalachian Highlands. The far eastern part of the state is located in the Ridge and Valley region. Valleys there can be steep and narrow, and the mountain peaks are high. The state's tallest mountain (and highest point) is Spruce Knob, which rises 4,861 feet (1,482 m) above sea level. Streams also cut through many ridges and form rugged canyons in the Ridge and Valley region.

The Allegheny Mountains are part of this region. Streams and rivers form deep gorges there. This hilly, rocky land is hard to farm. Instead, trees are a rich resource for logging, and coal, gas, and oil are mined. Most mountains in West Virginia are covered with trees, giving the landscape a rich, green look. The rest of the state is located within the Allegheny Plateau. In the western part of the Allegheny Plateau, the land gradually slopes down to the Ohio River.

YEAR
1859   Anti-slavery leader John Brown seizes weapons at Harpers Ferry in an attempt to fight slavery.
EVENT

- 13 -

Rivers crisscross all of West Virginia. Besides the Ohio, important rivers include the Potomac, Greenbrier, Monongahela, and Kanawha. West Virginia's rivers are home to more than 100 species of fish, including smallmouth bass, rainbow trout, and brook trout.

West Virginia does not have any natural lakes. Instead, lakes have been formed by dams on rivers. The dams provide hydroelectric power (electricity from falling water) and prevent flooding. Tygart Lake, in the northern part of the state, is one example of a man-made lake. Summersville Lake and Sutton Lake are located in the middle of the state.

Fishermen can take float-fishing trips down the New River Gorge (opposite), which is known for its stores of smallmouth bass and rainbow trout (above).

1861   Virginia breaks away from the rest of the U.S. at the onset of the Civil War.

Many animals are at home in West Virginia. Black bears, deer, and wildcats are found deep in the woods. There are plenty of cottontail rabbits, raccoons, skunks, and foxes. In the trees, cardinals, sparrows, and woodpeckers fly from branch to branch.

West Virginia relies heavily upon its natural resources. Although coal production had decreased by the 1970s, the state still ranks second in the country in terms of mining. West Virginia ranks ninth in salt production. Crushed stone, cement, sand, gravel, and lime are also mined.

Agriculture is important to West Virginia, too. The state has thousands of farms, many of which are located in the eastern panhandle, the north-central part of the state, and the Ohio River Valley. The leading crops are hay, grain, apples, and tobacco.

West Virginia is hot and humid in the summer and cold in the winter. The average summer high temperature is 85 °F (29 °C). In the winter, the average low is 22 °F (-6 °C). In the capital city of Charleston, yearly rainfall averages 43 inches (109 cm). Rain falls harder in the western Allegheny Mountains. Yearly snowfall ranges from 20 inches (51 cm) in the southwest to more than 50 inches (127 cm) in the mountains.

Raccoons often live in trees near a water source such as a pond or stream and hunt for food at night.

When coal is buried less than 200 feet (61 m) below ground, it is extracted using surface mining.

YEAR

1863   West Virginia separates from Virginia and becomes the 35th state on June 20.

EVENT

A Strong Work Ethic

BY THE TIME WEST VIRGINIA'S FIRST SETTLERS ARRIVED, FEW AMERICAN INDIANS LIVED IN THE AREA. THE FIRST WHITE SETTLERS CAME FROM EASTERN COLONIES SUCH AS PENNSYLVANIA, MARYLAND, AND DELAWARE. THE FIRST IMMIGRANTS CAME FROM WALES, SCOTLAND, GERMANY, AND SWITZERLAND. THEY WERE ALL ATTRACTED TO THE

Thomas Jackson earned his nickname when he would not abandon his position during a Civil War battle.

state's quietness and space. There was plenty of room for them to stretch out and start small farms. Later, when industry began, people from southern and eastern Europe came to West Virginia to live and work. West Virginians have always been known for their hard work, their quiet ways, and their desire for privacy.

General Thomas "Stonewall" Jackson, one of the most famous figures of the Civil War, was a product of West Virginia's emphasis on a strong work ethic. He was born in Clarksburg in 1824 but spent most of his adult life farther south in Virginia. Jackson began his career in the U.S. Army in 1846 and later served with the Confederate (Southern) army during the Civil War. He was considered one of the finest military commanders of the time, and his tactics are still studied by soldiers today.

The art of glassmaking by mouth and by hand has been practiced in the state since its early days.

YEAR
1873 The Chesapeake and Ohio Railroad is completed through West Virginia.
EVENT

No matter what kind of aircraft he flew, Chuck Yeager always named it after his wife Glennis.

Another military leader, Charles "Chuck" Yeager, grew up in Hamlin, West Virginia. He served in World War II as a pilot with the Air Force. After he returned home from the war in 1945, Yeager became a test pilot. In 1947, he became the first person to fly faster than the speed of sound.

Former National Aeronautics and Space Administration (NASA) engineer Homer Hickam was raised in Coalwood. His book *Rocket Boys* is about growing up in a coal-mining town. It was later turned into a 1999 movie called *October Sky*.

Olympic gymnast Mary Lou Retton is also from West Virginia. The Fairmont native won the gold medal in the individual all-around in 1984 when she was 16 years old. She was the first American woman to ever win a gold medal in gymnastics. Another famous athlete, National Football League wide receiver Randy Moss, hails from Rand. He attended college at Marshall University in Huntington.

In addition to the gold, Mary Lou Retton also won two silver and two bronze medals at the 1984 Olympics.

YEAR

1907 An explosion in the Monongah coal mine kills 362 people in the worst mine disaster in U.S. history.

EVENT

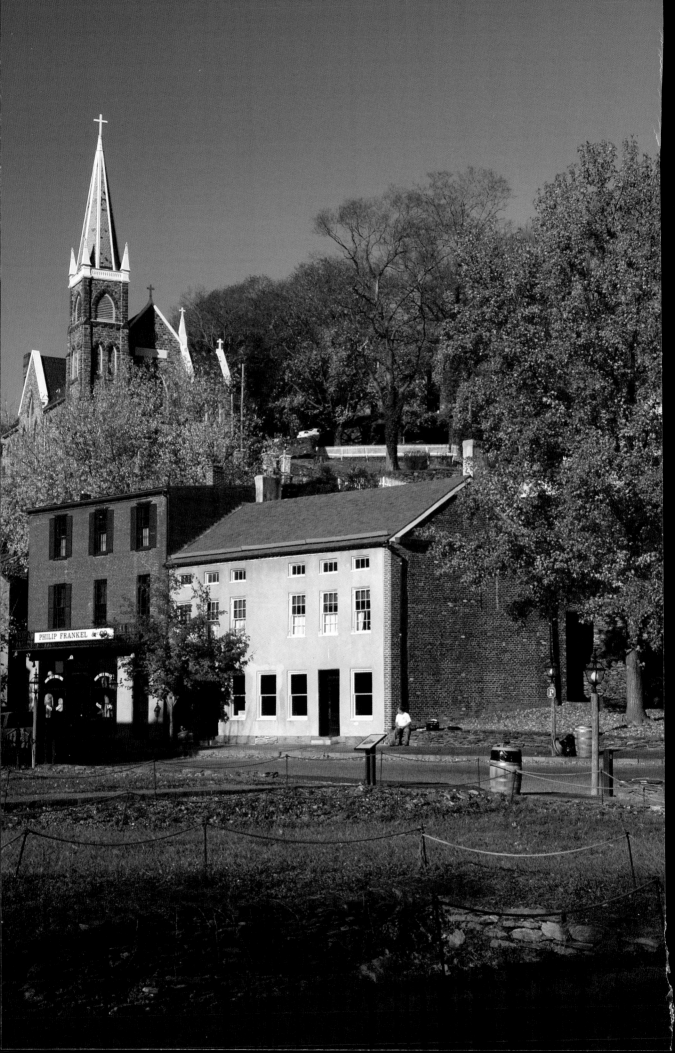

About 1.8 million people call West Virginia home. Most of the state's population is white. African Americans make up the next largest group, totaling about three percent of the population. Hispanics, Asian Americans, and American Indians make up smaller percentages.

The population of West Virginia is concentrated in the panhandles and in the south. West Virginia ranks about in the middle of all states in terms of population density, or the number of people who live in each square mile (2.6 sq km), with 75. But the state offers plenty of privacy, especially in the isolated central region.

Many historic buildings can be seen in West Virginia's peaceful towns (opposite and above).

YEAR

1954   The West Virginia Turnpike toll road is completed, providing a direct route between the Great Lakes and West Virginia.

EVENT

West Virginia's population peaked at two million around 1950. But then many coal mines dried up, and machines replaced human labor in other industries. Tens of thousands of people left the state. However, the population is starting to increase again, thanks in part to a thriving manufacturing industry. Many plants in the state produce chemicals, metals, transportation equipment, glass, and wood products. Thousands of people in West Virginia still work in coal mines, too. But jobs in government, education, and transportation now outnumber mining jobs.

Tourism is a growing industry in West Virginia. Visitors flock to the state year-round. In the summer, they raft on churning waters and hike in the mountains. They camp in the state's many parks. In the winter, they zigzag down powdery, snow-covered hills. Many people are needed to work in hotels, restaurants, and resorts to support the tourism industry.

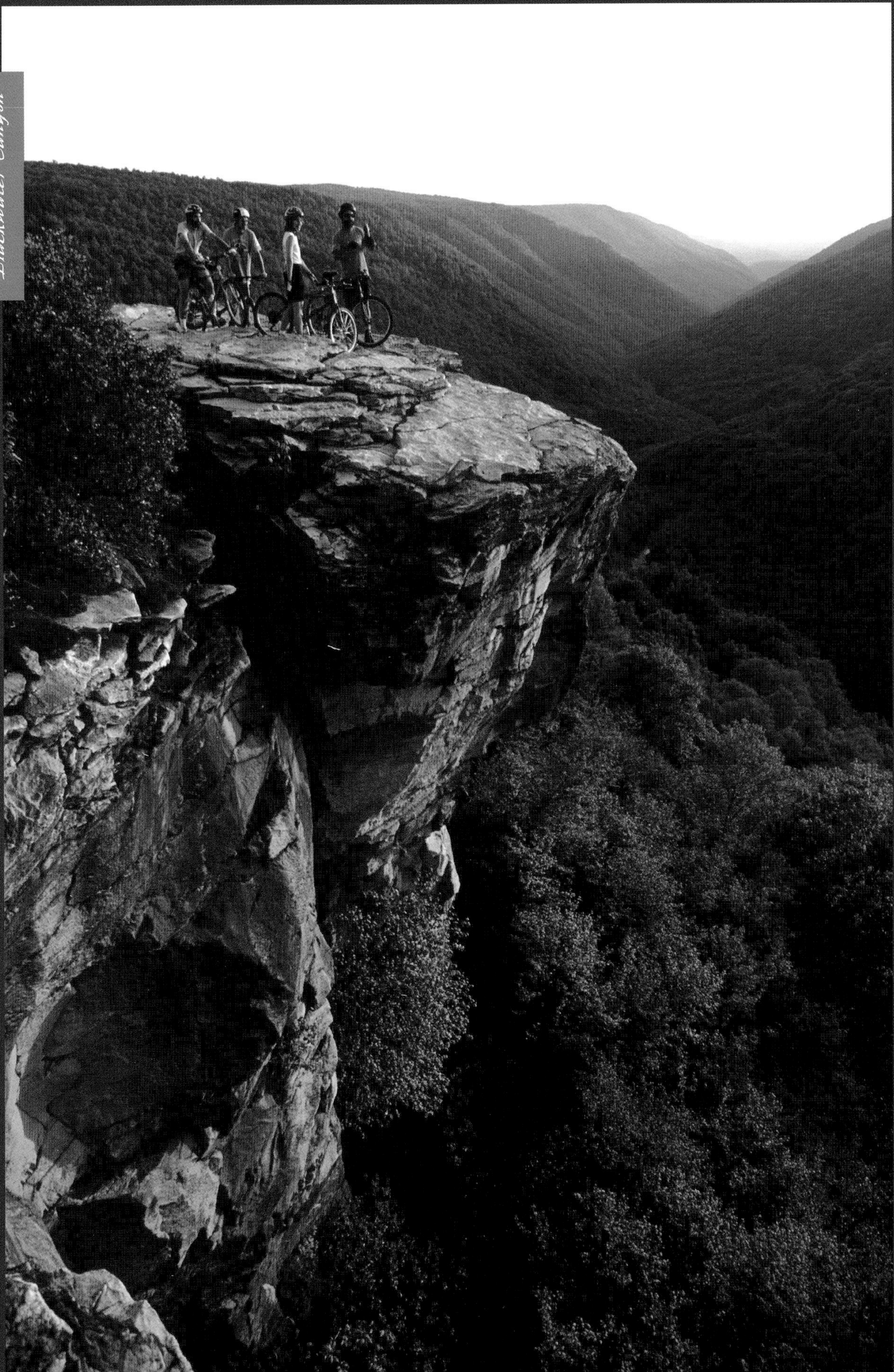
Blackwater Canyon

Legends and Beauty

With West Virginia's unique history, it's no wonder that the state is filled with stories and attractions. According to legend, John Henry was a former slave who worked on the railroad after the Civil War. At that time, workers had to blast tunnels through mountains. It was hard

work. Steam-driven drills made the job easier. John Henry claimed that he could dig faster than a machine. There was a contest, and he won. But his heroic effort killed him. No one knows for sure if John Henry was real, but a statue honoring him is located at the Big Bend Tunnel near Talcott.

Another famous West Virginia story is known to be true. After the Civil War, the Hatfield and McCoy families settled along the Tug Fork River. The McCoys lived on the Kentucky side, while the Hatfields lived on the West Virginia side. The two families had many disputes over land, property, and even relationships. The feud, which resulted in at least a dozen deaths, officially came to an end in 1891. Today, the region is a popular tourist spot.

Other tourist attractions in West Virginia are devoted to the history of the state's coal industry. At Beckley Exhibition Coal Mine, tourists can ride in small train cars and travel 1,500 feet (457 m) below the ground. They can also walk through a mining museum and see original miners' homes and other structures.

Those interested in Civil War history can visit a number of state parks that commemorate West Virginia's role in the conflict. Visitors to Droop Mountain Battlefield State Park

Every day from April through October, the Beckley Coal Mine is open for tours.

The gun-toting men of the Hatfield family did not get along with their neighbors, the McCoys.

YEAR
1967   The Silver Bridge in Point Pleasant collapses during rush hour, killing 46 people.
EVENT

- 27 -

can learn more about the site of the last major Confederate resistance in West Virginia in 1863. They can even follow trails through the places where soldiers once fought.

Those seeking a more adventurous destination can visit the New River Gorge Bridge on "Bridge Day," which takes place annually on the third Saturday in October. The steel-arch bridge is the highest bridge (at 876 feet, or 264 m) to carry vehicles in the Americas. On Bridge Day, the bridge closes to automobile traffic to allow thrill-seekers with bungee cords and parachutes to jump off the bridge for a wild ride.

West Virginia is known for calmer occasions as well. One of the most beloved holidays in the U.S. got its start there. When Anna Jarvis's mother died in 1905, Jarvis worked tirelessly to fulfill her mother's dream of honoring moms nationwide. Jarvis wrote hundreds of letters to lawmakers and executives. It took many years, but president Woodrow Wilson declared Mother's Day a national holiday in 1914.

As hard as West Virginians work, they also like to relax by watching and participating in sports and recreation. Even though the state does not have any professional sports teams,

The main span of the New River Gorge Bridge is 1,700 feet, the second-longest in the world today.

YEAR

1970   A plane carrying most of the Marshall University football team crashes, killing 75 people.

EVENT

- 28 -

YEAR

1977   The New River Gorge Bridge opens, becoming the longest steel-arch bridge in the world.

EVENT

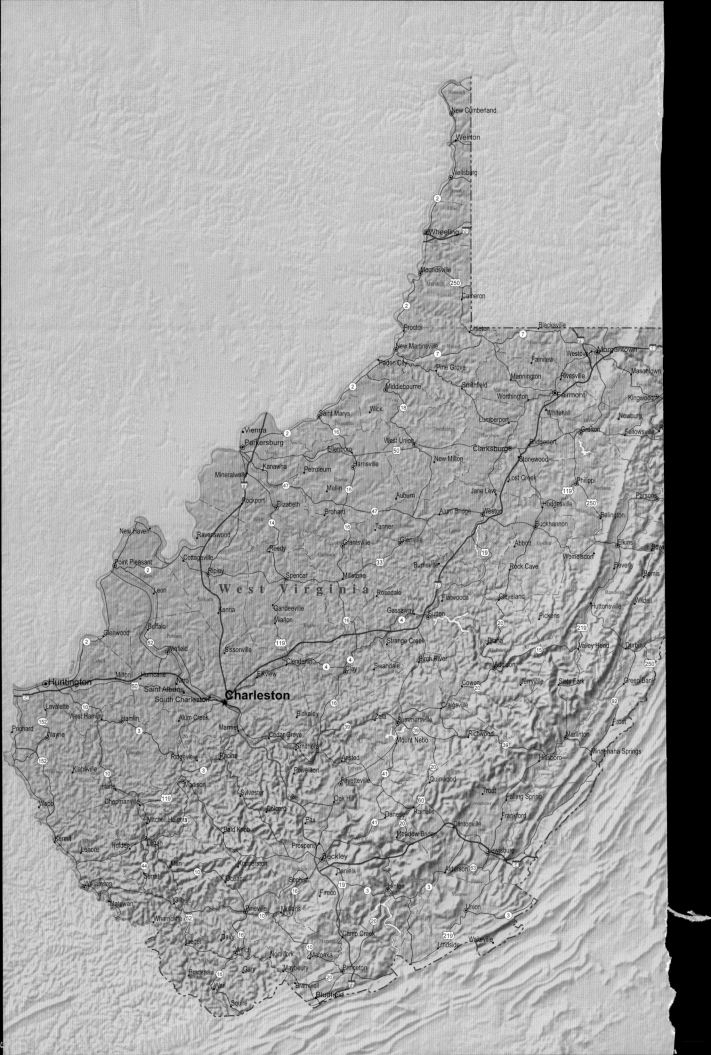

QUICK FACTS

Population: 1,812,035

Largest city: Charleston (pop. 50,478)

Capital: Charleston

Entered the union: June 20, 1863

Nickname: Mountain State

State flower: rhododendron

State bird: cardinal

Size: 24,230 sq mi (62,755 sq km)—41st-biggest in U.S.

Major industries: manufacturing, tourism, mining

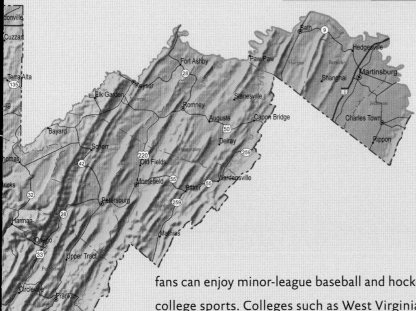

fans can enjoy minor-league baseball and hockey as well as college sports. Colleges such as West Virginia University and Marshall University often produce strong basketball and football teams. Many people also take advantage of the state's lakes and rivers to water ski and go whitewater rafting.

With its population on the rebound after years of decline, West Virginia's prospects are looking up. Jobs in manufacturing, mining, and tourism are helping the state recover from rough years in the 20th century. And its abundant natural resources are likely to attract people to the Mountain State for years to come.

YEAR

2006   A coal mine explosion in Sago leaves 12 miners dead.

EVENT

BIBLIOGRAPHY

Hopkins, Bruce. *The Smithsonian Guides to Natural America: Central Appalachia.* Washington, D.C.: Smithsonian Books, 1996.

Rice, Otis K. *The Hatfields and the McCoys.* Lexington, Ky.: University Press of Kentucky, 1982.

West Virginia Geological and Economic Survey. "History of West Virginia Mineral Industries—Coal." West Virginia Geological and Economic Survey. http://www.wvgs.wvnet.edu/www/geology/geoldvco.htm.

Williams, John Alexander. *West Virginia: A History.* Morgantown, W. Va.: West Virginia University Press, 2001.

Worldmark Encyclopedia of the States. Vol. 2. Detroit: Thomson Gale, 2007.

INDEX